Right After Sundown

Right After Sundown

Teaching Stories of the Navajos

By Marilyne Virginia Mabery

Navajo Community College Press
Tsaile, Arizona
1991

Copyright © 1991 by Marilyne Virginia Mabery

Published by Navajo Community College Press
Tsaile, Arizona 86556

International Standard Book Number: 0-912586-69-9
Library of Congress Number: 89-64113

Printer: Hindy's Enterprise, Hong Kong
Designer: Joanna V. Hill
Typeface: ITC Garamond

Printed in Hong Kong

Contents

Prayer from *The Navajo Night Chant*

In beauty, I walk.
With beauty before me, I walk.
With beauty behind me, I walk.
With beauty above me, I walk.
With beauty all around me, I walk.
With beauty within me, I walk.
It is begun in beauty.
It is begun in beauty.
It is begun in beauty.
It is begun in beauty.

Preface

I am proud to present this book in an effort to contribute greater understanding between young people of all cultures. This collection gives an idea of the cultural differences that exist between the Navajo and Anglo world views, and these differences are expressed in the variety of stories told by the Navajos.

I began research on Native American stories in 1973 and have continued to pursue deeper knowledge and understanding of them through the present day. This collection represents only the beginning of my efforts to communicate the oral stories of the Navajos, or *Diné*, "The People." Understanding of the traditional Navajo world view and philosophy is ultimately centered on their origin story of emergence into the present world. All stories, no matter how simple, stem from this basic one, being an elaboration or extension of it.

In this collection of twelve stories, I have condensed their ritualistic quality and have emphasized the simplicity, symbols, and morals of the stories. Numerous symbols are working within the stories and they appear in different guises such as Coyote, the Hero Twins, monsters, and the spirit beings, as well as many others. In this collection I have tried to use only one name for each of the participants. Each symbol is a representation of the real world, according to the Navajos. In order to introduce the reader to the oldest and most recent of Navajo stories, I have included origin stories, coyote stories, and a fairly recent one which describes a very recognizable place. In the Anglo sense, these stories may appear to be unrelated, but to the Navajos, they are all connected.

These stories are not colorful folk tales, or creative imagination of the writer, but are, for the Navajos, actual events. In their humor and graphic descriptions the stories seem to be folk tales. In their supernatural reality they take on the quality of legend. In their association with the complicated Navajo ceremonies, they explain and justify the moral values and cultural norms of traditional Navajo society. In their moralistic character, they represent the height of parable. Repetition, so customary in American Indian stories, is a reflection of the rhythms of daily life and the power of continuity.

I have added a comprehensive glossary of terms to assist the reader in identifying the monsters, peoples, spirits, and places described in the text. A bibliography is also included for those who desire further reading on the subject.

In collecting these stories I have relied heavily on out-of-print works by such researchers as Mary C. Wheelwright, in particular her *Navajo Creation Myth*; Margaret Ervin Schevill's *Beautiful on the Earth; Navajo Religion* by Gladys A. Reichard; "*Ise be' an yı* or Place Where There are Poles That Hold up the Rock" by Aileen O'Bryan, told in *The Diné—Origin Myths of the Navajo Indian*, and many more.

Several Navajo friends encouraged my early

research and because of their encouragement, I feel qualified to approach this subject. So many others provided support along the way, especially the librarians of the New Mexico State Library, the National Park Service research libraries, and others, by helping me revise and edit this work. To all these supporters, may they find this book to be a reflection of all that is beautiful in the Navajo way.

Finally, I would like to acknowledge several individuals for their help in researching this volume. In particular the State of New Mexico, Books by Mail Director, Ms. Carolyn Mathews and the Interlibrary Loan Librarian, Ms. Penny Grigsby, and their assistant, Ms. Helen Trujillo. I would like to give special thanks to the following Navajo people who were generous to share with me their people's oral history: Mrs. Mae Thompson, Mr. Andrew C. Charley, and Mr. Archie Werito. I am indebted to the Chaco Culture NHP Research Library, as well as El Morro National Monument's library. I feel I should also thank my husband, Ken R. Mabery, for his generous support and encouragement through the process of collecting, transcribing and proofing this volume.

Introduction

To the Navajos, everything is alive, and is a reflection of the Holy People. This is true not only for five-fingered beings, humans who walk upon the surface of the land, but includes the ants that crawl into the dark depths of the earth, the birds that soar above the highest peaks, the small stones found in a lonely arroyo of the reservation, and even the stars scattered across the sky. Each "living thing" is a representation of beauty, harmony, and balance; and all this is referred to by the word *hozho*. The Navajos believe that it is the responsibility of all to maintain *hozho*. . . . It can be lost very easily, and when that happens, a singer must help to correct the situation, and heal all involved, restoring *hozho*. Contrary to general western belief that the Navajos are not concerned with the individual, they are in fact deeply concerned with the plight and development of the individual. The wholeness of the human spirit itself, as it interacts with other individuals, as well as supernatural forces, creates harmony.

To the Navajos, an individual is responsible for its own development, and though the older generation will offer advice, it is always done in an indirect way. Maintaining harmony, balance and beauty in all that exists is the primary goal of discipline, and it is achieved with logic and self-control. It is not the Anglo logic that works here, but rather the more subtle grace of intuitive understanding. The Navajos do not lecture their young people about right or wrong. Instead, they tell a story to illustrate what they desire to teach, allowing the children to grasp for themselves what is appropriate behavior.

This collection consists of twelve stories grouped in two parts. The first section deals with the Five Worlds of the creation story. The second part contains stories of animals and characters who, through their own foolishness, made mistakes and suffered the consequences of their actions. All these stories express the traditional values of Navajo society and are a contribution to the greater story of the creation, emergence, and extinction of the human race. These stories are meant only as an introduction to the substantial oral treasures of the *Diné*, the largest tribe in North America.

Everyone who writes or tells Native American stories does so in a slightly different manner from another person, but the essence and truth of the stories remain unchanged. The stories have been passed down through generations, and the extensive cultural memory of a Navajo storyteller is almost incomprehensible to the ordinary Anglo person caught up in his television mini-series. Each story retold in this book was born in antiquity; the moral lessons are as valuable today as they were in the past.

Stories of the Beginning

The Beginning

When this world was young, everything shared a common language. The birds and beasts, the flowers and trees, all animals, like Slow Skunk and Long Nose Mouse, Gray Rabbit and Badger, were friends of the people. Even Old Man Mountain Lion helped them at one time, as did Coyote, the Schemer. But Coyote soon proved himself not entirely trustworthy and some things he has done since then have been questioned. In that long ago time the people lived as relatives of all the animals and plants upon the Earth, sharing common enemies.

It is hard to imagine how the Earth looked in that long ago time. Most of it was covered by water, and what was not was over-run by man giants. There were Tsédah odziltaalii, He who Kicks People down Cliffs; Horned Monster, or Deelgeed; Tseninahalee, the Monster Who Flew, or the Monster Bird. Hunger, Sleep and Lice were also enemies. The people lived in mortal fear of these giants and enemies.

The old, old storytellers say that finally the Monster-slaying Twins were born to do away with the giants and enemies.

There is not enough room in this book to tell you all the stories that the old ones tell children, but there is room to plant the seeds of their beliefs in your mind, and begin an understanding.

When the wind blows and begins to cool the Earth for winter, the stories are told. Each family gathers in the warm hogan to listen to their relatives tell ancient stories that are still important today. It is a time of crackling fires in the center of the hogan, a time to stretch out on the warm sheepskins and smell mother's mutton stew and fried bread. It is a time to be with one's family and to learn more about the wonderful world in which we live.

The Insect People

This is the story of the beginning of life. Long ago, the world was very different from today. Indeed, there was no world, no stars, no light. Yet everything was in motion. In time the energy became stars and worlds. And the Earth we live on was one of these, a part of the universe, different but still the same. There were no people as we know them, rather the world was inhabited by Holy People.

In the First World, there were Insect People. Some say there were seven in number, others say nine. They inhabited one small island that floated in darkness and around it were the four cardinal directions. From each of these directions certain things came to be. From the east came white cloud and daylight; the south, blue cloud; the west, yellow cloud; and from the north, black cloud and night. Everything that is now on the Earth came from these. Some things on the Earth are of dawn, others of twilight, others still of day or night. All exist in beauty and harmony. The surface of the First World was dark in color and the sun rose in the east as it does today.

In the waters surrounding the island, there lived four beings: Water Monster, Blue Heron, Frog, and White Mountain Thunder. These beings became angry at the Insect People for quarreling among themselves. They turned against the Insect People and commanded them to go elsewhere.

The Insect People knew of no other place to go, and they discussed the command for four days. On the fourth morning they saw a bright light in the east. Slowly the light grew toward the south, the west, and the north. The light was water, flowing toward them. The only way for the Insect People to escape the flood was to fly toward the sky. They watched the First World disappear beneath them. As they grew tired from flying around the sky, they saw a blue head appear in the sky. A voice called them, ''In here, to the east there is a hole.'' They entered the hole and emerged on the surface of the Second World. The blue creature who had brought the Insect People to safety was a swallow, and he lived in the Second World with other swallows.

The Insect People were fascinated by this new world, and they sent out scouts in the four directions to explore this world. When the scouts returned, they reported that they had seen no people like themselves in this world. Nothing existed but bare, level ground. The Insect People realized then that they were in the center of this place without food or friends. While the Insect People discussed this, the Swallow People came to find out why they had sent out scouts.

''We wanted to know what was in this world,'' was the reply of the Insect People.

''And what did your scouts tell you?'' asked the Swallow People.

''They told us that four times they came to the edge of your world. This world, unlike the First World, is blue in color and is filled with swallows, but no plants or other living things are on the land.''

"They spoke the truth," the Swallow People said. "Had you asked us, we would have told you this and saved you this trouble."

The Insect People said then, "You understand our language. You have legs, feet, bodies, and wings, like us. Can we live here as your friends and relatives?"

"If that is your wish," replied the Swallow People.

The Insect People and the Swallow People lived in harmony for a few days in the Second World. But soon the Insect People began to quarrel among themselves and with their adopted kindred. The Swallow Leader was very disturbed by the quarreling and behavior of the Insect People and called all of the people together and said, "We have treated you as friends and relatives and look how you have repaid our kindness. Your behavior here is not unlike your behavior in the First World and now you must leave this world too. This is our land and we will have you here no longer!"

When the Swallow Leader finished his speech, Locust decided to lead the Insect People into the sky. They circled it for a long time until they could no longer see the Second World. When they were against the hardness of the sky, they found no opening through it. As they began to tire and despair, they saw a white face staring at them. It was the Wind, and he told them to fly south where they would find a slit into the Third World.

The Third World was yellow in color and Grasshoppers lived here. Again, the Insect People sent out scouts in the four directions of the new world; and again they returned with stories of a yellow barren land inhabited only by Grasshoppers. When the Grasshoppers came to the Insect People, they consented to allow the Insect People to remain, and called them cousins.

As before, the Insect People were treated with great kindness and for a while they lived happily among the Grasshoppers. But soon they began to argue and act against the Grasshoppers and they angered their hosts. "You must go," said the Grasshopper Leader. "You were chased from the previous worlds because of such behavior and you have learned nothing. Be gone!"

Once again, the Insect People circled the sky. When they grew exhausted, a red head appeared at an opening in the sky. It was the Red Wind and he told them to fly to the west. The passage they found there was twisted like a vine. They flew in circles through it and came out into the Fourth World, along with Grasshoppers and four sparrows. The Fourth World was mainly white; the same colors were in the sky as in the previous three worlds. The Insect People saw four mountains in the Fourth World: one to the east, one to the south, one to the west, and one to the north.

Again, scouts were sent out to discover what was in this new world and they returned from their four migrations with different news than before. They reported tracks of deer and turkey and strange people.

The people cultivated fields and were gathering their summer harvests. The strangers had been kind and gave the scouts food—their names were Kisaani (Pueblos).

Now this land of the Kisaani had neither rain nor snow, but the people raised crops of corn, squash, and pumpkins. The Kisaani were willing to allow the Insect People to remain here. The Insect People gathered among themselves and decided that since the Kisaani gave them food and treated them kindly, they would change their ways.

Thus, the Insect People lived on the food of the Kisaani and were happy in the Fourth World. Everyone prospered and all were pleased with their condition. The Insect People hoped that they would not have to wander anymore.

Raymond J. Joanson

The Fourth World

Late in the autumn, after a voice called to the Insect People four times, four Holy People appeared. These Holy People did not speak, instead they made signs to the Insect People. When they left, the Insect People discussed the mysterious visit, and tried to understand what the Holy People had meant by their strange signs. On the fourth visit, one of them, called Black Body, remained to explain the presence of the Holy People.

Black Body said, "You do not understand our signs, so I will explain these to you. The Holy People want to make more people, but in a form like themselves. You have the bodies of insects and are unclean and smell bad. Clean yourselves before we return in twelve days." Then Black Body disappeared.

On the morning of the twelfth day, the Insect People were very excited. They had washed themselves and had prepared for the Holy People. The women had dried themselves with yellow corn meal and the men with white corn meal. Soon four Holy People appeared, carrying a sacred buckskin. They lay the buckskin on the ground in front of the Insect People, and also placed there two ears of corn, one white and one yellow, their tips to the east. Under the white ear, a feather of a white eagle was placed. Under the yellow ear, a feather of a yellow eagle was placed. The Holy People walked around the buckskin and blew wind upon it, causing the feathers to move. Soon the feathers disappeared. The Holy People lifted the yellow corn and First Woman stood up, and white corn was then lifted and there stood First Man. The four Holy People directed the Insects to build an enclosure of brushwood for the pair. First Man and First Woman were to live together as man and wife.

At the end of four days, the first set of twins was born to First Man and First Woman. At the end of four more days another set of twins was born. This continued until five sets of twins were born of First Man and First Woman.

Four days after the last pair of twins was born, the Holy People returned and took First Man and First Woman away to where the Holy People dwelt and kept them there for four days. When First Man and First Woman returned, all their children were taken to the hogan of the Holy People and were then returned to the Insects on the fourth day. First Man and First Woman and their children had learned how to represent the Holy People with the use of masks during this time. They were taught the right way to pray for rain and good crops. It is also thought that they were taught the use of tools.

With the return of the first family, the sons and daughters of First Man and First Woman married some of the Insects and soon there was a multitude of people on the land. These people looked the same as First Man and First Woman. At this time, all the Holy People and those people in the Fourth World were happy. Everything was harmonious in the Fourth World until eight years later.

One day the people saw the Sky dip down and

touch the Earth. At the point of contact, Coyote and Badger were born. Coyote was born first and as such is the elder brother of Badger; both are children of the sky and have special powers. As Coyote was being born, First Man told the people the sacred names of the Four Mountains which surrounded their homeland. When Badger was born he told the people of the four races of mankind.

Only days later First Man and First Woman began to argue. First Woman, confident that she was right, bragged about how well the women could survive without the men. First Man was so upset by the argument that he took all of the men with him to the opposite side of the river that ran through their homeland. During the first year of their separation the women did very well, living off the bounty of the fields which the men had planted and in the homes which the men had built. The men did not do so well, as they had to concentrate on hunting and had little time to build homes for themselves.

By the second year, things improved for the men. They had made new homes and found more game on their side of the river, and they planted new crops. But then the women were not doing as well. There was not enough food and the women's homes showed signs of needing repair. Yet First Woman did not give in and the people remained separated.

The third year passed and it was even harder on the women, while the men prospered. By the fourth year, First Man and First Woman realized that if the people did not come together soon, there would never be any more children. The men had become quarrelsome and bitter and the women were starving. Both men and women were performing unnatural sexual acts and the results were not good. First Man and First Woman knew this was not the wish of the Holy People.

First Man and First Woman reconciled. They brought all of the women and children across the flooded sacred river, except for one woman and her two young daughters. The woman was able to swim to safety, but her two daughters were claimed by Water Monster.

First Man and First Woman decided to go to Water Monster's house under the water to claim the two girls. Unseen by the pair, or the people, Coyote followed them. When First Man and First Woman entered Water Monster's house, they searched in three rooms before finding the children in the fourth room. Approaching Water Monster, they asked for the return of the girls. When Water Monster did not answer, they took the girls and walked away with them. Coyote, unperceived by all, took two of Water Monster's children and carried them out of the water under his robe. No one suspected Coyote of stealing Water Monster's children and everyone celebrated the reunion of the mother and her two daughters. The people were happy that their differences had been settled and that they had not been thrown out of the Fourth World, as happened in the three previous worlds.

The Great Flood

The next day all types of animals began to run past the people's village from east to west. The people grew concerned as more and more animals continued to pass for the next three days. On the fourth day the people saw a great light rise in the east. When the scouts returned at sunset they reported a great flood coming from the east.

The people called a council and it was determined that Squirrel could help them. Squirrel planted a piñon seed and a juniper seed but the trees did not grow high enough to save the people. Then Weasel planted a spruce tree, but this, too, stopped growing before it reached the security of the sky. Finally, as the water touched the ankles of the people, two men came forth, and the older one spread seven bags before the people. Each bag contained earth from the sacred mountains. The people begged help from the old man. He said he could not help, but that his son might be able to.

The people implored the man's son to help. The young man planted reeds in the mountain soil of the bags. The people saw the roots of the reeds sticking out of the soil, and they grew rapidly downward. A moment later all the reeds joined together and became one reed of great size, with a hole in the center. The young man instructed the people to climb inside the reed. Just as the hole closed behind them, they heard the sound of water rush over.

Soon the people in the reed came to the sky. They sent Hawk to find a way into the Fifth World. Hawk returned exhausted and then the people sent out Locust. Locust was gone a long time but when he returned he said he had found a place in the Fifth World for all the people.

When the people entered the Fifth and current world they were in the center of a great body of water. The leader threw out four turquoise beads into the lake so that it would drain. When the water

was gone, the people saw a great white land to the east. Their island was connected to a mainland.

The people rejoined and celebrated over the new land. The Fifth World was more beautiful than the previous worlds and the people were thankful that they had been saved. But Coyote threw a cloud on their happiness when he told them that it had not been a good thing for the people to live forever. He told them that if this continued, there would be no room for the children of the people. The people saw the wisdom of Coyote's words and became silent. Since that day, people die daily and their spirits join with the Holy People.

On the fourth day after emergence into the Fifth World, someone returned to the hole from which the people had come and saw that much water was seeping into the new world. First Man rose and studied the problem, then turned to Coyote. "There is a rascal among us! I believe that it is Coyote. He has stolen something from Water Monster's house."

The people tore off Coyote's robe and found two children of Water Monster. At once First Man threw

Water Monster's children back into the hole of emergence, and the water receded from the new world and rushed back into the lower world. But with the flood water many monsters had entered this new world. The people saw them and were frightened, yet there was so much room in their new world that they decided not to be concerned. From the place of emergence, the people spread out across their newly found world, multiplying and living productive lives in harmony with the creatures around them.

The Monster-slaying Twins

The Monster-slaying Twins, or Monster Slayer the elder, and Born-of-Water the younger, played a large role in every major event that happened to the people in the early part of the Fifth World. They were strong and handsome.

There were many monsters in the new world. One Walking Giant, or Ye'iitsoh La'í Naaghaii, lived at Hot Springs, and ate people who came there at twilight to bathe. The twins waited beside the cave where One Walking Giant was known to live. Born-of-Water hid behind a boulder at Hot Springs while Monster Slayer hid on the east side of the cave, overlooking the lake, and waited.

Some time passed before Monster Slayer saw the giant's head stick out of the cave. Ye'iitsoh stood up and then saw the twins. He said, "What are these two beautiful things that I see? I shall kill you two and eat you."

The twins answered "What is the beautiful big thing we see?"

They repeated this four times between themselves, confusing the giant. On the fourth repetition, they sprang forward and killed Ye'iitsoh.

The twins left the lake and walked toward a red flare in the distance. Quietly, they found a doorway and entered the cave from where the flame seemed to come. Here they found many kinds of monsters.

Immediately one of the monsters spoke, "Grandsons! Why would you want to kill us? I am Hastiin Dichin (Mr. Hunger) and the others are Poverty, Sleep, and Lice Man." The voice echoed around the twins four times and then Hunger and the others jumped on the twins and beat them almost to death.

Sometime later when the people found the twins, they were in terrible condition. A meeting was held to decide how to help the twins. Raven was at this meeting, along with many others. At Raven's suggestion, a healing dance was held over the Monster-slaying Twins, and they finally recovered.

As soon as they were well, the twins set out once again. This time they found a monster named Tsedahodziltalii, or the Monster-who-kicks-people-over-the-cliff. He was a monster who appeared harmless and pleasant because he looked human. The twins found him asleep, sneaked up on him and kicked him in the knees. When Tsedahodziltalii was unable to stand they took their knives and easily killed him.

Still feeling strong, they went in search of Horned Monster. Horned Monster had excellent eyesight and and whenever he saw a person, he charged at the person and ate the person alive. The twins used their magic to make themselves invisible, and with the tips of a lightning fork, they blinded Horned Monster before killing him. But as they killed Horned Monster, Monster Bird attacked them. The older twin ducked behind a boulder and shot the bird with two magic arrows, saving his brother from certain death. The first arrow struck the Monster Bird on the right side, the second arrow hit its heart. Immediately the Monster Bird turned into an eagle and an owl.

By this time the twins were very fatigued. They discussed their condition and the number of monsters still remaining, and decided to ask Changing Woman, their mother, for help in fighting the monsters and saving the people.

How Navajoland Was Formed

Changing Woman is one of the most beloved of the Holy People. She renews herself each time she grows old.

She received five hoops from the Monster-slaying Twins. These hoops were magic and were meant to destroy the beast and monsters who had made trouble after the emergence into the Fifth World. Changing Woman walked to the east and set the black hoop so that it would roll. Then she spat through it with spittle of black hail and nudged the hoop forward. At once it rolled over the hill to the east and was lost to sight. Then she took the blue hoop to a place in the south and set it so it would roll. She spat through it again, this time with blue hail, and the hoop rolled out of sight to the south. Carrying the yellow hoop to a place west of the village, she spat through it with yellow hail, and the hoop soon rolled out of sight into the western distance. Finally, she carried the white hoop north where the Monster-slaying Twins were waiting. Again she spat through the hoop with white hail spittle, then with a gentle nudge she sent this hoop on its journey.

The fifth hoop, which was many colored, she threw straight up into the air and it sailed skyward, soon lost to sight in the noon-time zenith. Once it disappeared, she threw five colored knives in the same direction, blowing a powerful breath after them.

Up they flew until they too disappeared. As the hoops and knives vanished from the sight of the people, dark clouds formed in all four directions, filling the heavens. Thunder bellowed and rumbled all over the sky, and the earth was soon covered in darkness. Overhead, thunder cracked, from the north it rolled, from the south it echoed, and from the west it rumbled. Never before had such a sound been heard and never has it since. The clouds grew and mingled until the world was so dark that noth-

ing could be seen in the darkness. A strange light grew slowly in the west but it was not as bright as a sunset.

Changing Woman saw all this happen and said nothing. The people cried in fear, but still she said nothing. The twins became anxious but Changing Woman would not console them. The Earth began to tremble under their feet and at last Changing Woman motioned for the twins, the people, and animals to follow her into her hogan.

On the fifth day, the sky cleared and there began four days of good weather. But once again the sky grew dark, and a thick white cloud descended on the earth.

Changing Woman went outside at last to look around. She observed the effects of the violent weather everywhere she looked. Huge whirlwinds were so fierce that they had uprooted trees, and giant boulders were tossed around like grains of sand.

Who could live through such winds without magic, she wondered? Neither monsters nor humans were safe from the forces she had released upon the Earth. She returned to the hogan, looked upon the people, and called the twins to her side. She said, "My sons, I fear for the people and for this home. We live too high in the mountains, and the great winds will surely destroy this place."

Seeing Changing Woman's fear, the twins went outside to find a way to protect the people. They observed the thick black clouds overhead, and taking out their knives, cut a large black cloak from the clouds and covered the dwelling. They fastened a thick blanket of fog over the house with sunbeams. Deciding to make certain of their magic, they covered the dwelling several times. They secured each layer with sheet lightning and then chain lightning. Then they re-entered the hogan to wait out the fury of the storms.

The storm continued for four more nights and four more days, never ceasing in its fierceness. Hail such as none had ever known fell upon the Earth; rain soon saturated the Earth crust and floods began to cut into the sides of the mountains.

The people cried in constant fear, but Changing Woman remained stout, coaxing them with these words, "Surely, the weather is our friend. Not even monsters can survive such wind, such hail, such earth shaking."

On the morning following the final, most violent night, everything became silent and calm. Changing Woman and the twins went outside to make sure the storm was over. As the twins removed the protective coverings from the hogan, Changing Woman called the people outside to see the results of her magic. The people stood in awe, for as the coverings drifted skyward the sun shone brightly on the Fifth World. It had never been so lovely.

Everywhere the Earth and Sky were filled with color. A soft, warm rain descended and slowly removed from the Earth the evidence of violence that had so changed it. A rainbow grew from horizon to horizon, blessing the new land and the people, and their brothers, the animals.

Everyone marveled at the changes the storm had made. Where once there had been only four mountains with a wide valley in between, there now were deep canyons crisscrossing the Earth. Stark bluffs and flat mesas rose in the distance. Mountain grass had replaced the bare soil of the valley. A new terrain had been hewn which gave the landscape the shape and character the Southwest retains to this day.

"Surely the monsters who emerged in the Fifth World have been destroyed," said Changing Woman. "No one could have lived through the fierceness of such forces."

The people agreed with her. They were all thankful that they were spared and that the Earth was such a place of bold beauty.

The Messenger Wind now whispered to the hero twins, "There are still four monsters left. Their names are Old Age Woman, Cold Woman, Poverty, and Hunger."

The next morning, the twins set out towards the northern mountains. After a long journey, they met an old woman coming slowly toward them. Recognizing Old Age Woman they waited until she came alongside them. When she noticed them, Born-of-Water said, "Grandmother, we have come on a tragic errand. We have come to kill you."

"Why kill me?" asked the old woman. "I have never done harm to anyone. I have heard of your great deeds, Monster-slaying Ones, and I know you have killed the other monsters in order to increase mankind. But if you kill me, there will be no increase of the people. The old people will never die. Children will not grow up to become parents. The people will stand still. It is best that people should grow old and die. Let me live, and I will help to increase the people."

Monster Slayer thought she was a very wise old woman, so he encouraged his twin to spare her life. Born-of-Water agreed and quietly the twins went back to Changing Woman's hogan.

The next day they sought out Cold Woman in the high peaks where the snow never melts. Here they found a very lean, old woman sitting on the snow without shelter or food, fire, or clothing. Her eyes streamed with icicles, her teeth chattered as she shivered. Only snow birds flew around her as the wind howled. Born-of-Water shouted above the roar of the wind, "Grandmother, we have come to kill you. The people suffer from the sickness you send in the winter time. Too many die at your hand." And he raised his war club to strike her.

Cold Woman said to the hero, "You may kill me or not, just as you will. But if you kill me it will always be hot. The land will be dry, the springs will cease to flow. The people will be thirsty from heat. It would be better to let me live."

Monster Slayer took the club from his brother and thought about the woman's wise words. Once again the brothers agreed not to act. They left the mountains and returned home.

When the Messenger Wind whispered to the twins that Poverty still lived, Born-of-Water asked Changing Woman how to find this monster. She refused to tell him. The wind whispered once again. Once more the twins followed its heavenly voice to the place where an old man and old woman sat on Waterless Mountain.

They were in tattered clothing, dirty, owning nothing between them. The elder twin spoke this time, "Grandmother and Grandfather, we are sorry, but we must be cruel to be kind. We have come to kill you for the sake of the people."

"Grandchild," said the old man, "It would be unwise to kill us. In the days to come your people would always wear the same clothes and never get anything new. If we live, their clothing will wear out, and the people will make new and beautiful garments. They will gather goods because they will have to work. Let us live so that we can have their old clothes. Born-of-Water nodded to his older brother and together they left the old couple alone.

Hunger was still living and the brothers discussed this as they made their way to Changing Woman once more. As neither could see any use for Hunger, they agreed to find the monster and destroy it.

They listened to the Messenger Wind the next morning and followed it to a place where there was a large area of white grass. Here they found not one but twelve Hunger people. Monster Slayer said to the leader, "Understand why we must kill you and your people. It is necessary so that our people will never suffer the pangs of hunger again." He lifted his bow and pulled the string tight.

Just before the arrow flew, a Hunger Person spoke. "It would be foolish of you to kill us,

Monster-slaying One. If we die, the people will grow to dislike their food, and soon will complain and grow bitter. If you want the people to increase, you must let us live. We are truly your friends. If we go, men will no longer learn the rewards of good hunting, or know the pleasures of cooking and eating good things."

The twins lowered their weapons and slowly made their way home. They realized that some of the monsters were necessary to keep the world in balance. When they arrived at Changing Woman's hogan, they laid their weapons to rest. They told the people in song how all the monsters were now dead; only those necessary to strengthen the people were still alive.

"Hozho! All is in balance. All is beautiful upon the Earth. All is harmony once more," they sang and the people joined in.

Stories of the Fifth World

The Fifth World

Many more adventures took place in the building of the Fifth World. Many characters took part in those stories. There is a story for everything that came to be in all of the five worlds, and if you are a Navajo you will hear some of these stories in your lifetime they say.

You may understand some of these stories, but not others. You will remember some of the stories and forget others. What needs to be remembered is remembered. What speaks to you is for you, what is not for you is not needed. For each person, what is needed to live is here. What is not needed is for someone else. What is needed to survive for each individual will be different, yet the essentials are for everyone, and everyone will remember these things. It has always been this way and will continue forever.

The next six stories deal with lessons to be learned. Coyote has always played a role in teaching lessons to the young. That is his role and he happily maintains it. Though he isn't punished in the stories, his stumbling nature is meant to be humorous and to graphically demonstrate the error of his reasoning. "Big Long Man and the Mountain Lion" is a transition story, taking place just before animals and man could no longer speak to each other. "Coyote and The Twins" is a story of change brought on by the Holy People to further the world in its cycles. The last story is of Niwhilibiihi, "The Gambler"; it brings us almost to the present time.

RAYMOND J. JOHNSON

The Origin of
Little Black Stinkbug

This is the story of the stars and planets, and the role one small creature played in molding the heavens as we know them today. Just as a child speaks with childish words, so his thoughts reflect his growth, and so it is with all the young creatures of Earth. Our leaders were not born with great wisdom; wisdom comes slowly with age and size. Stinkbug, too, was very young and foolish in the beginning.

After the people arrived in the Fifth World the Holy People first decided the heavens should be created and they allowed Black Body to use crystals to make the stars. BLack Body had a helper who kept the order of the stars and planets. This helper was known as Little Beetle, Chief Star Keeper, Companion of the Morning and Evening Stars.

The night sky was then a thing of great light, with rows of well-arranged stars. All the stars had been so well placed by Black Body that night was like day without sunlight; starlight was brighter than the full Moon.

Little White Beetle began his job each evening as soon as the Sun retired with Changing Woman to her home in the west. First, Little White Beetle began to pick up the stars from his basket. Tenderly and affectionately, he cleaned and shined each star before putting it in its proper location in the evening sky, beginning in the east and working toward the west. By the time he reached the western sky, a joyous array of starlight filled the heavens. In this way there was never a moment of darkness upon the land, for without light the dwellers of earth are doomed to a limited experience.

Before dawn each day Little White Beetle began to pick up the stars and place them in their basket. Tenderly and affectionately, he tucked them away for the night to come. He was always orderly and methodical, so as not to misplace any star or planet. By the time the Sun rose over the eastern

hills, Little White Beetle was finishing his job on the far western horizon. His timing was always superb.

As years went by, with night following day, Little White Beetle began to tend his basket less carefully, confident he was more favored than his other brothers upon the Earth. He bragged about the sparkling sky as if he had created it, saying "If it wasn't for my work, man would lose the enchantment of the night sky, and the night creatures would mourn their fate." The Holy People saw what was coming, but they always left their children to work out their own problems, seldom interfering unless called upon for assistance.

One evening, Little White Beetle was bragging about his wonderful creation, and entirely forgot to watch the sun dip beneath the western horizon. Snatching up his basket, he raced to the eastern sky. But it was already dark—so very dark—and White Beetle could not see where to place the stars. A few stars he managed to place properly. These are now known as Man with Feet Ajar (*Scorpio*), Revolving Male (*Ursa Major*), Revolving Female (*Ursa Minor and Cassiopeia*), Slender First One (*part of Orion*), Pinching or Doubtful Stars (lower branch of *Hyades*), Rabbit Tracks (near *Canis Major*), and finally *Dilyehe* (or the Seven Sisters). Then oops!... he tripped over Coyote, who was feeling left out because Black Body had not consulted him about White Beetle's conduct. Coyote had already decided to make sure that Little White Beetle didn't get away anymore without being corrected. Little White Beetle tumbled onto his back, spilling his basket of stars and planets across the sky. Some stars formed the Milky Way, or the Path of Spirits, and others were scattered randomly across the sky. No longer was the sky as bright as day, even when the Moon gave its full brilliance once every 28 days. Thereafter, the sky was cloaked in velvet black for most of the month, even to this day.

The Holy People decided to visit Little White Beetle. "My child," they spoke, "you alone had a very special job in creation, a job suited to your natural talents of order and arrangements. Each of my children has been given an equal job to fulfill with joy! Each one of you was created with special abili-

ties to complement another. We have also hidden a challenge within your hearts. We have placed in it a seed which reflects ourselves. With this you will discover yourself and see us reflected in all of creation. You will see us in the nighttime and in daylight, in the clouds, the rocks, the flowers, and the trees, even in the birds who soar across the sky.

"Everything has been given power to reflect our qualities. From the ant and the bee you will see the talent of working hard. From the flower you may learn of color and harmony, and from the spider you shall learn weaving. The rhythm of music may be learned from the wind and the songs of birds. By seeking out the special talents of each other you will help one another, and thus learn your own natural abilities. He who serves his brother, whether bee, flower, man or beast, serves the Holy People.

"See Little White Beetle, your job was indeed special, for it brought inspiration, joy and light to all living things. Yet no one is more important than another in creation. All must work together in joy and harmony, for only without pride or envy can happiness live within you. By setting yourself above the others you have failed yourself, and us, in your task. You have reflected your failure in all of creation. Because of your conceit, the rhythm of day and the night has been forever disturbed. You have plunged the sky into semidarkness, and made this a part of Earth's experience.

"Therefore, from this day forward your shining white back will be as black as the night you made, and your brothers will remember this for the rest of your days.

"Go now, and tell them the paradox of creation. Tell them light and dark are like twins, like night and day, like man and woman. The power which gives life is the same power which will take back life. Tell them their own thinking will guide them on the path towards us or away from us. They are to give up pride and conceit and foolish desire. Then with us all will dwell where it is said, 'In beauty it begins, and in beauty it ends!'"

Thus ends the story of Little White Beetle, whose coat was once shining white but who is now commonly referred to as "Little Black Stinkbug."

Coyote and the Rain

My friends, I see you have come once again to hear more stories of the Navajos. As you saw in the last story, Coyote is a prankster; he always looks for trouble and usually finds it. As a result, Coyote is in trouble most of the time, but thanks to his magical powers of everlasting life given to him when he was born, he is able to come back to life and try again. One of the marvelous things about Coyote is that he never learns from his mistakes. He is always trying to trick someone out of something and to take what doesn't belong to him. Whenever a Navajo elder corrects a child, he usually adds a tale of Coyote to reinforce the lesson. I now will tell you several stories of Coyote to let you see for yourself what a rascal Coyote can be!

Coyote was jogging along one day. Everything

was suffering from heat, the very rocks were scorched red and dry by the powerful rays of the sun. Coyote wiped his brow and panted from the heat. Looking into the sky, he saw it was crystal clear, there were no clouds anywhere.

"I'm so hot," he complained. "I wish a little white cloud would come along to shade me." Instantly a white cloud appeared. However, it was not large enough to shade Coyote.

"I wish a much larger cloud would come," Coyote said. "I wish there would be a little breeze to cool me."

A large cloud appeared and a breeze cooled Coyote as he continued on his way, but it was still too warm for Coyote, and he was not happy with the world yet.

"I wish it would cloud up everywhere," he cried, "so there would be no sunshine to warm me. I wish the breeze would become a wind and sweep across the whole earth."

Immediately these wishes were granted, and Coyote was so pleased that he made yet another wish.

"I wish a few drops of rain would fall," he said, "just enough to moisten the earth." Rain fell and soon his hair became wet, but still Coyote wasn't satisfied.

"I wish a gentle shower would cover the earth," Coyote said, "so the soles of my feet would be cooled as I trot along." Once more his wish was granted, but Coyote was not satisfied with this either.

"I want wet sand to ooze between my toes, and water to rise past my knees and shoulders." The rain came down harder, and soon the water was deep enough to swim. By this time a real flood was in progress, moving down the arroyos and washes. Once again Coyote asked.

"I want to float down the stream to some animals' homes, like a prairie dog town," he laughed. "I want to catch all of the little drowning animals I can."

The water roared higher and moved very swiftly downstream, carrying Coyote. Pretty soon Coyote found that the water was moving too fast. He struggled to keep his head above the mass of muddy water, but the water had collected all types of sticks and brush in its haste to grant Coyote's wish. Coyote splashed around in panic, forgetting to keep his head above water. Soon he was swept into a prairie dog town. When the storm was over and the waters receded, the little prairie dogs came out of their holes to look at what the storm had left behind. They found the dead body of Coyote. So they called Vulture to take his carcass away.

RAYMOND J. JOHNSON

Coyote and the Otters

Coyote is always happiest when he is able to pry into someone else's business. One day as he jogged along, he spied a group of young otters playing. They had made a mud slide and were taking turns climbing the grassy bank above the water, pointing their heads toward the lake and sliding gaily into the water. It looked like great fun to Coyote!

Coyote trotted over and sat down to watch the game. The otters pretended not to see him; they went on about their play as if he were not there at all. Coyote did not like being ignored. He moved closer and began to talk to the youngest otter.

"That looks like fun," he said, "what do you call your game?"

"It's called sliding."

"Sliding, huh?" Trying hard to be friendly,

Coyote smiled, "Do you mind if I join you?" All the other otters looked at him coldly.

Finally the oldest said, "You are not an otter, Coyote. Go play your own games. We don't want to teach you our game."

Coyote smarted from the sting of the young otter's word. "It wouldn't take me long to learn your game," Coyote replied, still trying to be friendly. "All I have to do is lie on my belly and slide into the water." He inched closer. "Let me try it just once."

"Our game is very dangerous to anyone who doesn't live in the water. You enter the water very fast and you must hold your breath until you reach the bottom, then somersault and swim to the top. Otherwise you will drown."

Coyote didn't believe a word of that. He had seen the young otters surface every time they slid down the slide. None of them had drowned, so why should he?

He begged the poor otters four times and finally, so that he would leave them alone and let them continue their game, they agreed to allow him to try.

"You can try it," said the oldest otter, "but only once. Then you must go on your way and let us play. Also you must not blame us if you are killed when you cannot hold your breath long enough to swim back to the surface." Coyote was already on his belly lining up to shoot down the slide. He didn't listen to the elder otter's instructions, and forgot to hold his breath as he careened wildly down the slide to the water. Coyote didn't see the sour looks exchanged by the otters as he hit the water. He was happy that they had allowed him to play.

He made a beautiful belly flop as he hit the water, his long nose pointed down into the water. Down, down, down he went and still he went down. All of the time Coyote never tried to swim or do the somersault the young otters had told him about. When he reached the bottom of the lake he cracked his head on a giant rock and was knocked unconscious.

The otters waited for Coyote to surface. Finally, after a long time the eldest otter shook his head.

"Coyote did not listen to our warnings. I think he

must be dead. Let us continue our game." The youngest otter took his place at the top of the slide and slid into the water. When he surfaced he told his brother about Coyote lying at the bottom of the lake.

"He is lying directly in our way," said the young otter. "It is very dangerous for him to be lying there."

"Poor, foolish Coyote," the elder said. "I guess it isn't right that we should just leave him there. But it is going to be hard work to bring him back up to the surface."

The youngest otter spoke up, "It would be easier to bring him back to life and make him swim on his own."

"That's a very good idea," the elder replied, "come on kids!" Together they jumped into the lake and swam to the depths of the lake. Forming a magic circle around Coyote they performed their own secret magic on him and brought him back to life.

"Now go!" the otters said in unison. "After this don't try to play otter games. We don't want this to happen to you again."

Coyote and Badger

Coyote was jogging along in the country when he met his brother, Badger.

"Where are you going to so slowly, brother?" Coyote asked.

"I have friends in Big House. They will get supper for me. Do you want to go along?"

Coyote is always hungry, so he nodded his head and accompanied Badger.

The people at Big House were friendly. They cooked food for both their guests. Badger was very shy and only ate a little, but Coyote ate all he could.

The people waited until the two of them had finished eating, then said, "Coyote and Brother Badger, we will let the one who brings us the most rabbits marry our daughter." Coyote liked this, as he had been eyeing the pretty daughter while he ate. He decided right then and there that he must marry the girl, and to do this he knew he was going to have to trick his brother. During the night Coyote prayed for snow, and the next morning the world was cloaked in white.

Coyote left the house very early, tracking rabbits. He was able to catch one young rabbit who tripped, but all of the others ran into their deep burrows, and he could not dig deep enough to pull them out.

"I'll dig them out," Badger volunteered. Coyote moved out of the way and watched his brother's long, sharp claws dig at the rabbits. Soon Badger had piled up a stack of big healthy rabbits.

Coyote ran around chasing all of the rabbits into their burrows. Then he called Badger to dig them out. He smiled to himself as Badger became tired from working so hard. When Badger had dug deep into one burrow, Coyote rolled a giant rock over the hole, blocking Badger's exit.

"He can't dig out from under that," Coyote bragged. Picking up the rabbits, he hurried to the home of the people to claim the pretty daughter.

"I've brought you all of the rabbits in the neigh-borhood," he told the people. "Now I will marry your daughter."

"We must wait for Badger," the people answered, knowing that their daughter preferred Badger to Coyote.

Poor Badger. He was very tired and though he pushed and pushed, he could not move the rock Coyote had rolled over him. Finally he gave up trying to push his way out of the hole and dug in the opposite direction. He didn't get to the people's house until after dark.

"Why are you so late?" asked the people.

"Coyote placed a rock over me while I was digging," Badger told them.

"I would never do that to my brother," Coyote lied. "Badger is making that up to win the girl."

But the people knew about Coyote's tricks. They gave their rabbits to Badger, telling him that he had won their daughter, and could marry her the next day.

Coyote was very angry so he built a great fire to keep the day from coming. But finally the sun peeked over the mesa, and everyone awoke and started the marriage ceremony.

Coyote went to the maiden and asked, "Wouldn't you rather marry me, pretty girl, rather than my brother, Badger?"

The girl laughed. "I would never marry *you*, Coyote. I could never even like you."

Coyote was shocked. He couldn't understand why the girl would like his shaggy brother better than him, but since she did, he decided he might as well go on his way.

Coyote and the Monster-slaying Twins

Once, two Navajos disappeared. The people looked everywhere for them but they were not to be found. The people said to Coyote, "Child-of-Skyblue-You-of-Eternal-Life, please look for the twins Monster-slayer and Born-of-Water."

Coyote nodded and set out searching. At this time a great council was called for all the Holy People. They were to meet for a very long time, for there was much to say and many important things to decide. The meeting concerned the Moon and the Sun; the length of the day and night; winter, summer, spring, and fall; how age should follow youth in all beings; the path the Sun should take across the sky; the number of stars to spread across the heavens; the number of planets; and much more. Coyote was one of the first born, and as such was considered a holy person. He felt he should be at the meeting, yet he knew the people would be angry if he did not find the twins.

Coyote decided to make something that would locate the twins while he attended the meeting. He tied a rope to a giant rock and threw it into the lake known as Black Water Lake. As he watched the rock disappear, he said, "When this rock emerges from the dark water, the twins will be with their people again." So saying he left and went to the meeting of Holy People.

When he arrived there, the Holy People were talking about the separation of the animals; the deer, the rabbit, the bear, the mountain lion, and mankind. Coyote didn't like the sound of the changes, and he wasn't sure he liked not being able to know what the other animals and men were thinking if these changes came about.

He listened as it was discussed that each animal would live with its own kind, and that they would speak only among themselves, that there would be special breeding months; each species would have babies, and some would be born in a nest, some on the ground, others inside shelter, and each should have parents whom they resembled.

Each thing was being put in order, according to its own natural niche. As the vote was called to decide these things, it was already starting to get light, a new day was beginning, and Coyote knew he must check on the rock. He ran with all of his supernatural speed to the lake. He could see nothing. By the time he returned the vote had been taken and he had to accept the new conditions.

The Holy People were now discussing the placement of flowers and other plants. Coyote became bored with this talk and went to sleep. He didn't vote on the kinds of water, trees, or sagebrush there should be and where they would be placed. When he woke, it was another day of the council, and he raced to the lake in order to check on the rock. Again he saw nothing.

The meeting of the Holy People continued as Coyote returned. They were deciding on medicines; there would be male and female medicines.

Each would grow in different places and be used for certain ailments. Their uses would be taught to the Navajos as needed.

So many things were being changed, thought Coyote, that he decided to remain here on the third morning instead of checking on the stone. But he sent the Wind to the people to ask that a man and a woman go check on the rock in the lake.

When the couple looked into the water, there was a giant hole, the Emergence Hole, where they could see all the way down into the First World. Nothing was at the bottom of the hole, so they decided they should contact Coyote and ask about this magic.

The meeting continued. It was established that adults would know all of the things decided at the meeting, and these things would be taught to children as they became adults. They discussed how teachers should begin, and whom should teach what. It was decided that as old age came to people, so would wisdom. This would be the gift given to the young by the old. The elders would know the ceremonies and the way of the worlds. They would know the names of the stars, and directions. It is still that way.

The couple who went to the lake called Coyote from the meeting and told him what they had seen. Coyote told them to go back and look again. And so they did. This time when they looked into the hole, they saw the twins for whom they searched at the bottom of the hole. They called to the twins but the twins did not respond, so the couple went back to Coyote.

The Holy People had now created things of twelve and named them and placed them in order. They created twelve months, twelve holy songs, twelve prayers, twelve cycles of the moon, and twelve phases of each cycle of the moon.

All things would follow the laws set down by the Holy People at this meeting, and Coyote knew he had been wise to stay at the meeting rather than try to find the twins.

The couple returned and asked Coyote why the twins did not respond when called. It was Coyote's job to impart the meaning of the decisions made at the meeting to the couple. He told them that from that day on the twins would remain in the shadow world of the Holy People, just as all things must now follow the new rules of the Holy People. He turned and joined the Holy People. Since then no animal has spoken to man, nor has a Holy One approached man except in dreams.

Big Long Man and Mountain Lion

The old people say that long ago it was not uncommon to see men and animals talking or walking arm in arm. Everyone was friends. One day Big Long Man was walking like this with Mountain Lion toward Red Lake. When they came to Big Tall Pine, Mountain Lion challenged Big Long Man, saying, "I can climb better than you!"

Big Long Man did not answer as he peered into the branches of the tall pine. He glanced at Mountain Lion and then began climbing. Mountain Lion was annoyed by the confidence of Big Long Man. He pushed past Big Long Man and beat him to the top of the tree. Big Long Man continued climbing, never halting and being cautious all the way. Mountain Lion called down to Big Long Man, "Look, look at me, Big Long Man," he bragged.

Big Long Man frowned at such boasting. He finally came along side Mountain Lion and said calmly, "I may not be able to climb as fast as you, Mountain Lion, but I can climb anything you can."

Mountain Lion laughed loudly and reached out his big paw, slapping Big Long Man in the face. Big Long Man fell backwards. This made Mountain Lion laugh even harder. Just as he was about to call down to Big Long Man, he felt a jerk on his tail. Big Long Man had caught his tail and was pulling Mountain Lion out of the tree. The two tumbled together toward the ground.

Mountain Lion screamed and cursed, his words offending Tall Pine Tree. Tall Pine spoke, "It is bad to use swear words, Mountain Lion." He said, "I will not help save you in your fall; instead I will help Big Long Man who climbed fairly." Pine Tree caught Big Long Man in his branches, but Mountain Lion fell to the ground and was killed.

Big Long Man jumped out of the tree unhurt, and quickly skinned Mountain Lion. Since that day, Navajos have been good hunters.

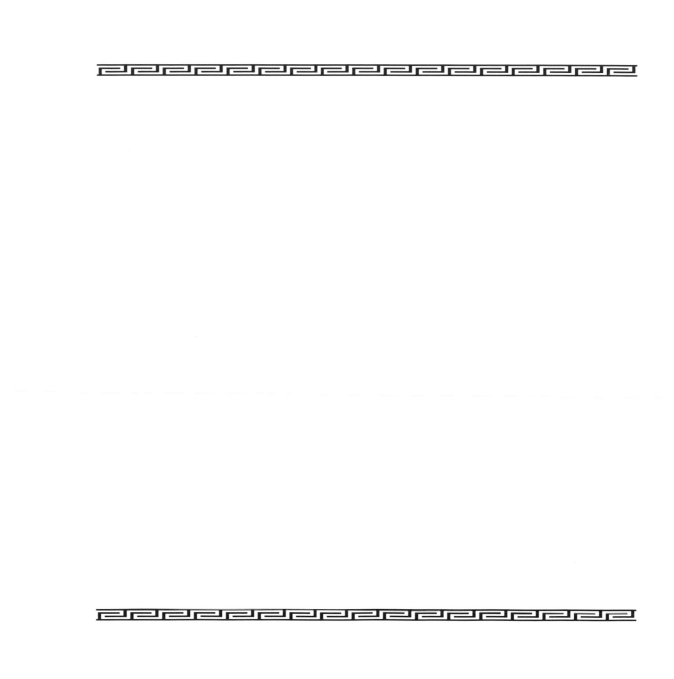

Niwhiilbiihi,
The Gambler

This will be the last story I will tell you, my new friend. It is a story of not so long ago, and it happened in a place that is easy to find.

Once, in the canyon now known as the Chaco, there lived a man nicknamed Niwhiilbiihi, or the Gambler. Niwhiilbiihi was very lucky in all of the games; even as a boy he won at anything he tried. As he grew to be a man, his family told him he must go out on his own and make his own life.

He left his home far to the south and journeyed many days to find the great canyon he had only heard about. He knew that many people lived there and he was anxious to gamble with these new people. When Niwhiilbiihi found Chaco he was overcome at first by the richness of the people. He decided to bide his time and learn all he could about the people before he gambled with them.

Niwhiilbiihi was adopted by a widow and was treated as her son. He lived in the great Pueblo Bonito. The richness of the inhabitants continually amazed him. He was growing very anxious to teach these farmers the art of gambling.

Finally, one evening in the kiva he taught the members of his adopted clan a new game. It was called the basket game. Six flat dice, white on one side and black on the other, were used. If all six dice fell with the white side up, then the player won. The game was very popular with the men.

Niwhiilbiihi was very shrewd and lost almost all of the throws at first. Soon after the men were familiar with the new game Niwhiilbiihi introduced five other ones. Each time he was careful never to win too often. And the games grew in popularity until the entire pueblo was playing his games.

Finally, Niwhiilbiihi decided the time was right. He began to win all the games he played. Pretty soon the people of the pueblo had gambled away their household possessions, then their fields, then their laborers in those same fields, and finally members of their own families. The gambler had become very rich—the richest man in the pueblo.

But this did not satisfy Niwhiilbiihi. He wanted more. Soon the whole Chaco Canyon community, over twenty pueblos and small villages, had begun to gamble with him. Very quickly Niwhiilbiihi won everything in the canyon and on the high mesas above it. He was the richest man living, all the people had become his slaves. Still he had to gamble.

During this time a Navajo woman was taken captive by Niwhiilbiihi and was forced to work for him. She was given only scraps of food from Niwhiilbiihi's meals, and was forced to go about naked except for a grass apron. The only ornaments she had were a few turquoise and bone beads she had been wearing when she was found. The small children of the village constantly made fun of her, following her around and throwing stones at her.

Subjected to this daily harassment, the woman grew angry and bitter. Finally, she climbed the steps on the cliff behind the pueblo. Standing at the top, she shouted down the cliff to the people of Pueblo Bonito saying how horribly she had been treated. She reminded them that she was human too, and that they had given her no bed to sleep in, no food to eat, no clothes or ornaments to wear. She shouted bitterly of the children's harassment, and the laughter her presence had caused. Then she took off her few beads and holding the string above the people, she cursed Niwhiilbiihi for being such a horrible leader to them. She said that soon all the residents of the canyon would be like her; poor slaves to a master that craved only gambling. She dropped her beads and a great crack appeared in the rocks hovering above the pueblo. Then she disappeared.

Two years after the Navajo woman's disappearance from the cliff, a young man came into the pueblo. He was very handsome and a good hunter. Soon he became a great favorite of the town. But he would not participate in the gambling. This bothered Niwhiilbiihi so he set spies upon the young man, but no one ever caught him gambling.

One evening the strange boy caused strong winds to blow. The boy collected a young woman from each of the twelve clans in the pueblo and went to the home of Niwhiilbiihi. When Niwhiilbiihi asked the boy four times what he wanted, the boy told him he was the son of the Navajo slave woman, and that he had come to win back the freedom of the people who lived in th canyon. This made Niwhiilbiihi laugh, but since the boy was so brazen he decided to gamble with him.

The boy wagered all twelve young women against twelve young men that Niwhiilbiihi brought forward. They threw the dice four times and on the fourth toss the dice all fell on the white side for the boy. Then Niwhiilbiihi said, "Let us play a different game."

The boy wagered the twelve young women and the twelve young men against the same number of people chosen by Niwhiilbiihi. Again the boy won and again Niwhiilbiihi said, "Let us play a different game." In the end the two played twelve different games, each time doubling the stakes of the wager until the Navajo boy had won all the people from Niwhiilbiihi.

After the boy won all of the people, he set them free. They were happy and rejoiced. After the feasts they scattered to the four directions from whence they had first come, abandoning the canyon and great pueblos of Chaco Canyon.

The boy then told Niwhiilbiihi that he must join him in a journey to the Sun. Niwhiilibiihi and the boy rose like birds and disappeared into the sky, never to be seen again. Silence as well as beauty was restored to the rock canyon now known as Chaco.

Prayer from *The Navajo Beauty Way*

Hozoni

Come upon the trail of song,
O, Beautiful upon the earth
Where everything is in accord
Within, Without.
Happily may all men regard you
As you return to your home,
The old men and the old women
The young men and the young women
As you go to your home in the west,
To the home of Turquoise Woman
On the island in the west.
Happily may all your powers
Be restored to you.
Crossing the old age river,
I see you
On that wide, white water,
In Old Age
Walking on the path of beauty
Where all is Peaceful.
All is peaceful, indeed.

It is finished in beauty.
It is finished in beauty.
It is finished in beauty.
It is finished in beauty.

May all my words be acceptable to you.

Navajo Glossary

Navajo Vowel Pronunciation
a, as in father
e, as in net
i, as in like
o, as in so,

Vowels may also be nasal, some may have a high tone, others a low tone, rising tone, or falling tone. Whenever vowels are long, they are written as: aa, ee, ii, oo

Badger Second animal born of the Sky; Coyote's brother, good hunter, shy, modest.

Black Body Holy Person who explained the roles that the Insect People would play in the Fourth World. The creator of stars from crystals.

Black Cloud Created in the First World and lived in the North.

Blanca Peak The easternmost boundary of Navajoland in Colorado, near the headwaters of the Rio Grande, south of Great Sand Dunes National Monument, northeast of Alamosa, Colorado.

Blue Cloud Created in the First World and denotes South.

Blue Heron One of the four original Holy People is in the First World.

Born-of-Water Youngest of the twins, children of Changing Woman. One of the Monster-slaying Twins, his brother is Monster Slayer.

Changing Woman Holy Person who can renew herself each time she grows old. Mother of the Monster-slaying Twins.

Chaco Chaco Canyon, now a National Historical Park in northwestern New Mexico.

Cold Woman One of the monsters that plagued the People in the Fifth World, argued successfully with the twins for her life.

Coyote First-born animal of the Sky—known as Child of Dawn-Skyblue-You-of-Eternal-Life. Trickster, and prank player. Brother of Badger.

Dineh or Diné Navajo word for themselves, means "The People."

Dintetah Original homeland of the Navajos in northwest New Mexico and Colorado.

Emergence Hole or Place of Emergence Place where Insect People emerged into each world, exact location unidentified in current literature.

Fifth World The current world.

First Man Created from white corn and a white Eagle feather by the Four Spirit Beings in the Fourth World.

First Woman Created of yellow corn and a yellow Eagle feather by the Four Spirit Beings in the Fourth World.

First World Black world where the Insect People lived.

Frog One of the original four people of the First World.

Grasshopper People People of the Third World who welcomed the Insect People.

Hastiin Dichin Hunger Monster who convinced the Hero twins that he should remain.

Hero Twins The sons of Changing Woman. Older twin named Monster Slayer; younger twin was Born-of-Water.

Hogan Home usually with five sides, dirt floors, made of stone or wood.

Holy Ones Holy People who never die. They came enclosed in the universe at its creation.

Holy People See Holy Ones.

Horned Monster or Deelgeed Monster with exceptional eyesight.

Hozho Term meaning all is well, all is peaceful, all is beautiful, all is as it should be.

Hozhoni Term meaning harmony, balance in all things.

Insect People Mentioned in the First World.

Kisaani The Pueblo people.

Kiva Ceremonial or meeting chamber used by the Pueblos.

La Plata Mountains Sacred range of mountains in southwestern Colorado where Mt. Hesperus is considered the northern sacred mountain.

Monster Bird One of the monsters of the Fifth World. When killed by the Monster-slaying Twins, turned into an eagle and an owl.

Monster Slayer Oldest Son of Changing Woman; is brother of Born-of-Water.

Monster-slaying Twins Children of Changing Woman. Oldest was Monster Slayer; younger was Born-of-Water.

Mount Hesperus Northern sacred mountain—southern Colorado between Durango and Cortez, Colorado, defines boundary of Navajoland.

Navajo Largest tribe in United States.

Navajo Mountain A sacred mountain on the far northwestern corner of Navajo reservation, not one of the four boundary defining mountains.

Niwhiilbiihi or The Gambler or The One Who Always Wins.

Old Age Woman One of the monsters in the Fifth World. Responsible for aging in humans. Successfully argued with the Hero Twins for her life.

Poverty One of the monsters in the Fifth World. Responsible for giving people new things and goals to work toward.

Pueblo General term for many southwestern tribal groups who live in apartment-type towns.

San Francisco Peak Mountain range near Flagstaff, Arizona, western sacred mountain, defining Navajoland. Humphrey Peak is identified as the southern sacred mountain.

Second World The world of the swallows.

Squaw Dance Part of the Enemyway ceremony, a social dance rather than a religious dance.

Swallow People Blue people inhabiting the Second World, allowed the Insect People to remain until they caused trouble.

Third World The world of the Grasshoppers.

Tsaasi The yucca.

Tse Biyah Anii a hi Pueblo Bonito or more properly: "Village Where The Rock Is Braced Up."

Tsedahodziltalii He Who Kicks People Down Cliffs Monster or He-Who-Kicks-People-Over-Cliffs, in the Fifth World. Killed by the Hero Twins.

Tse Ninahaleeh Monster Bird, or the Monster Who Flew.

Water Monster One of the original beings of the First World.

White Cloud Existed in the First World to the east.

White Mountain Thunder One of the four Holy People in the First World.

Ye iitsoh One-Walking-Giant, in Fifth World and was killed by the Hero Twins.

Yellow Cloud Existed in the First World to the west.

Bibliography

Callaway, Sydney M. and others. *Grandfather Stories.* Navajo Curriculum Center Press, 1974.

Haile, Father Berard. *Upward Moving and Emergence Way.* Santa Fe: Museum of Navajo Ceremonial Art, 1942.

Hogner, Dorothy Childs. *Navajo Winter Nights.* New York: Hale, 1938.

Judd, Neil M. *Material Culture of Pueblo Bonito.* Washington, D.C.: Smithsonian Institution, 1954.

Kluckhorn, Clyde and Leighton, Dorothea. *The Navajo.* 4th Ed. Cambridge: Harvard University Press, 1962.

Locke, Raymond Friday. *The Book of the Navajo.* Mankind Publishing Company, 1976.

Lyons, Paul Jones. *Blue Feather.* Prairie Publications, 1953.

Moon, Shelia, Ph.D. *A Magic Dwells*. 1st Ed. Wesleyan University, 1970.

O'Bryan, Aileen. *The Diné—Origin Myths of the Navajo Indians*. Bureau of American Ethnology. Washington, D.C.: Smithsonian Institution, 1956.

Pousma, Richard H. *He Who Always Wins*. Grand Rapids, Michigan: Government Publication, Conf. Pub., 1934.

Rock Point Community School. *Between Sacred Mountains*. Rock Point Community School, 1982.

Rossel, Robert A., Jr., and Platero, Dillian. *Coyote Stories*. Rough Rock, Arizona: Navajo Curriculum Center, 1974.

Schevill, Margaret. *Beautiful on the Earth*. Santa Fe, New Mexico: Hazel Dreis Edition, 1947.

Vilasenor, David. *Tapestries in Sand*. California: Naturegraph Company, 1963.

Wheelwright, Mary C. *Eagle Catching Myth, Red Ant Myth*. Santa Fe, New Mexico: Museum of Navajo Cermonial Art, 1942.

Wheelwright, Mary C. *Navajo Creation Myth and Wind Chant and Feather Chant and Myth of Mountain Chant*, 1946-51.

Williamson, Rau A. *Living the Sky; Cosmos of the American Indian*. Houghton Mifflin Company, 1984.

Willoya, William and Brown, Vinson. *Warriors of the Rainbow*. Healdsburg, California: Naturegraph, 1962.

Wyman, Leland Clifton. *Beautyway: A Navajo Ceremonial*. New York: Pantheon Books, 1957.

Yazzi, Ethelou. *Navajo History*. Navajo Demonstration School, 1973.